Contents

Preface

What an exceptional destiny was that of Matilda! Born in Flanders in the castle that belonged to her father, Count Baldwin V, she was introduced to William of Normandy who she was later to marry around 1050. She was far from imagining, on her wedding day, that she would one day be the Queen of a kingdom as powerful as, if not more than the Kingdom of France or the Holy Roman Empire. From her union with William, she gave birth to at least ten children, two of whom were to become king. Designated Regent of Normandy during the Norman Conquest, she was later crowned queen of the new Anglo-Norman Kingdom, thus becoming one of the most influential of William's companions.
Whilst living a wise and exemplary life, this queen of legendary discretion, managed to assert herself among her contemporaries, for whom she was an abiding source of praise.

CHRONOLOGY

Circa 1032: birth in Flanders of Matilda, daughter of Baldwin V of Flanders and Adele of France.

1050: marriage with William Duke of Normandy, celebrated in the town of Eu.

1051-1052: birth of her son Robert, known as Robert Curthose.

Circa 1055: birth of her son Richard.

Before 1060: birth of her son William, nicknamed Rufus.

Circa 1061: birth of her daughter Cecily.

Before 1062: birth of her daughter Agatha.

Mid-June 1066: William gathers together his barons at the Château de Bonneville and names Matilda

Matilda's Normandy

MONUMENTS, RESIDENCES AND SITES VISITED BY MATILDA

Regent of Normandy for the duration of his expedition to England.

18th June 1066: consecration of the Ladies' Abbey in Caen, richly endowed by William and Matilda

10th September 1066: embarkation of the fleet.

Before 1067: birth of her daughter Adele.

1st September 1067: death of her father Baldwin V.

6th November 1067: beginning of the second Regency of Normandy, accompanied by her son Robert, now aged 15.

11th May 1068: Matilda is crowned Queen of England. At the end of the same year, birth of her son Henry, nicknamed Beauclerc.

1073: death of her daughter Agatha.

1075: death of her son Richard.

14th July 1077: consecration of Bayeux Cathedral in the presence of William, Matilda and their children.

1080: marriage of her daughter Adele to the Count of Blois.

1st November 1083: death of Matilda in Caen.

A prestigious line of descendants

A glorious genealogy

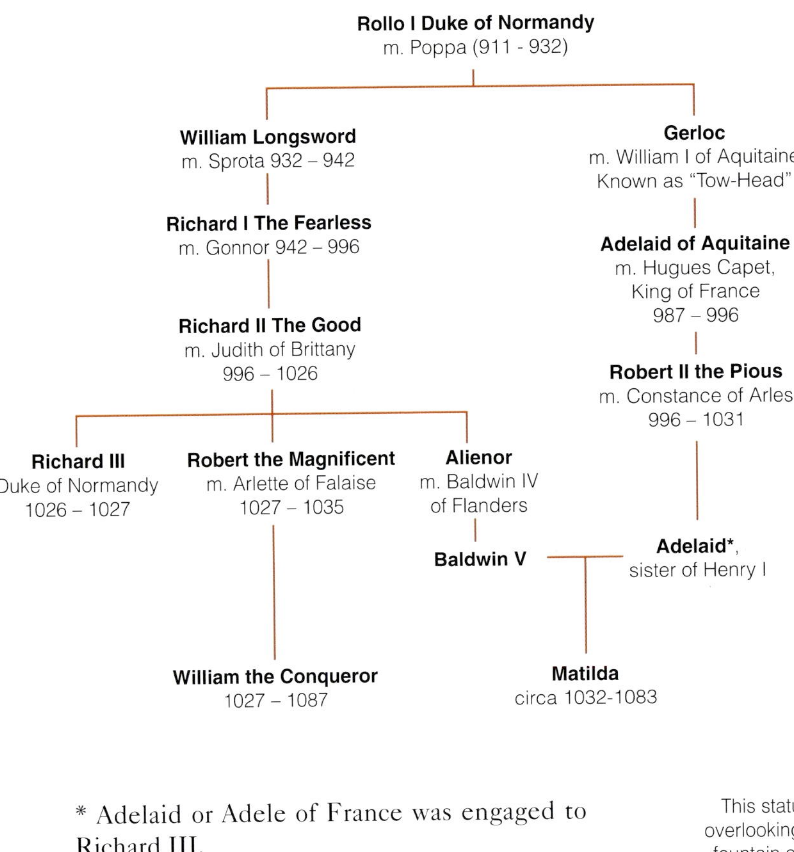

* Adelaid or Adele of France was engaged to Richard III.

This family tree clearly demonstrates the family links between William and Matilda. They were related in two ways: they were both descendants of Rollo, family ties having crossed when Richard III was engaged (or perhaps married?) for a few months to Adele of France, and Baldwin IV was married to Alienor who was William's aunt. One can also find Matilda's royal origins.

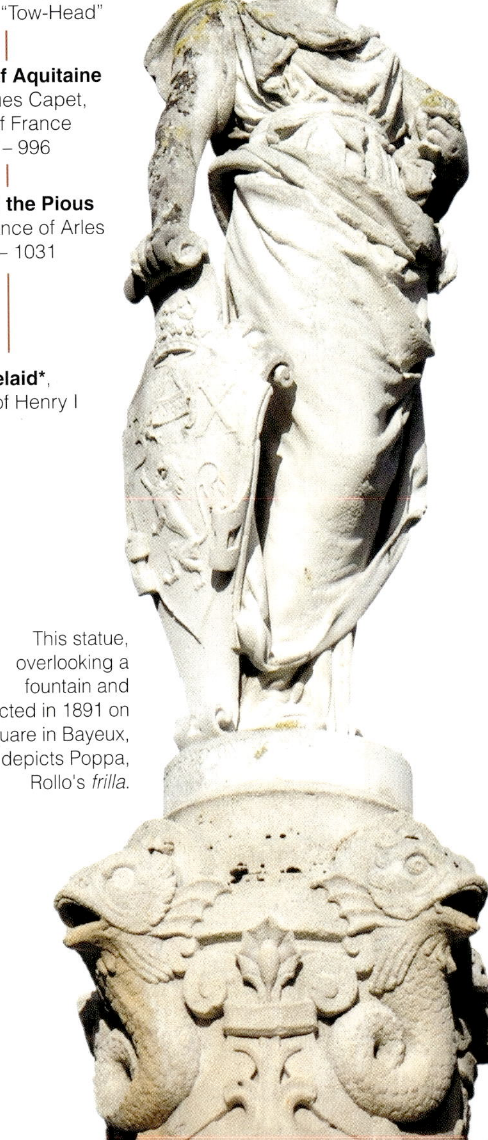

This statue, overlooking a fountain and erected in 1891 on a square in Bayeux, depicts Poppa, Rollo's *frilla*.

Her ancestors

Matilda had several origins, some of which largely exceeded the prestige of the County of Flanders, and of which her family tree clearly bears evidence. Retracing the ancestors of this discreet queen is in a certain manner, a way of rebuilding France's history from the Middle Ages and beyond. Matilda was a direct descendant of "Walker Rolf", a Norwegian pirate chief. After the death of Charlemagne, the Frankish kings were helpless faced with the surge of Scandinavians approaching their coasts and rivers, and ravaging villages and monasteries on their way inland. Tired of these devastating raids, King Charles the Simple decided to meet with Rolf at Saint-Clair-sur-Epte in the year 911. He offered Rolf his own territory to the East of the Seine, on the double condition that he become his vassal, and that he keep watch on the coasts against further pirate incursions. Rolf also accepted to convert to Christianity thus adopting the name of Rollo. His Christian marriage with the daughter of Béranger, Viscount of Bessin, was simultaneous to his union with his "frilla", or concubine named Poppa who gave him many offspring. One of their daughters, Gerloc, gave birth to Adelaid of Aquitaine, future wife of the King Hugues Capet, who founded the Capetian dynasty which reigned in France up to the French Revolution. Hugues Capet's son Robert II the Pious married Constance of Arles, who then gave birth to Henry I (later King of France) and Adelaid, who married Baldwin V, with whom she mothered Matilda. Such prestigious origins made Matilda not only the descendant of the first Duke of Normandy but also of the founder of the Capetian monarchy. On her father's side, her ascendants were just as noble. Baldwin V was a direct descendant of Baldwin II, who was the son of Baldwin Iron-Arm and who created the County of Flanders in 883.

The youth of a princess

We know very little of her childhood or of her family's place of residence which may have been in Flanders, Lille or even Ghent? It is however possible, thanks to the accounts of chroniclers of the same period and archaeological works, to trace a portrait of this quite extraordinary queen. Her father, Baldwin V, was the powerful Count of Flanders and her mother, Adele, daughter to the Capetian King Robert II the Pious, thus making Matilda the niece of King Henry I of France. Just like all young girls born from nobility, young Matilda was offered an excellent education, worthy of her rank: religious instruction, reading and writing, initiation to embroidery. This schooling offered Matilda solid general knowledge and remarkable manual dexterity, which is quite evident on the autographic charts[1] preserved in archives in Normandy and England, showing her signature in the form of a Jerusalem cross at the foot of each text. The outline of the cross branches shows the great regularity she applied in producing it: a fine line with no smudges and that is evocative of her dexterity in the use of a quill. Chroniclers of Matilda's era, and later illustrators, described Matilda as being a tall and beautiful woman, which certainly denotes their legitimate respect for the queen, but does not necessarily appear to be based on the truth. Prudence would rather value archaeologists' findings. Excavations undertaken by Michel de Boüard in 1961 gave way to the opening of Matilda's tomb and a detailed study of her remains carried out by Professor Dastugue, Director of the Anthropology laboratory at the Caen University Hospital. These studies revealed that Matilda was in fact a small and frail woman, no taller than 1 metre 50 (4 feet 11 inches).

1 Autographic charts: texts bearing the signature of William and Matilda.

Matilda and William's Wedding

Drawings of William and Matilda based on a fresco that adorned a former chapel in the Men's Abbey.

A political union

Having learned that Baldwin of Flanders had a daughter named Matilda, of noble origins and character and of delicate beauty, he[2] asked for her hand in marriage after consulting his counsellor (William of Poitiers). In the 11th century, there were only two possible outcomes for a young girl like Matilda: marriage or the convent. Her parents chose marriage. The young girl was at the centre of major political stakes for both families. Baldwin, her father, firmly intended to take control of maritime trading in the North Sea, in particular with the English, thus infuriating the Emperor of Germany, who was far from supportive of such expansionist aims. Then came a propitiously timed and promising alliance between the Duke of Normandy and King Edward of England, known to be a Norman ally. For William, who had long since endeavoured to abate the dishonour brought by his illegitimacy, the perspective of marrying a princess of royal blood intesified his interest in Matilda. Such a union would be the ultimate revenge against the Richardides[3] and would bring William closer to the King of France, his suzerain[4], for whom he would become a nephew-in-law. The young couple met around 1050, at Eu, a town on the border between eastern Normandy and the neighbouring County of Ponthieu.

Two entwined pelicans
– a symbol of Christian union.

2 William.

3 Richardides: name given to the direct or indirect heirs of Duke Richard, all of them claimants to his succession, and who did not consider the bastard William to be worthy of the Duchy of Normandy.

4 Suzerain: feudalistic term. A suzerain is a high-ranking lord to whom a lower-ranking lord, called a vassal, owes "faith, homage and obedience" and in wartime provides him with soldiers.

They were both very young; William was 23 and his young fiancée barely 18. William was immediately captivated by the young girl who, according to the chronicler William of Jumièges, was "of a very beautiful body and a generous heart". He was to love her faithfully until his death, which, at that period in history where concubines were rife and annulments blessed by the church, was quite exceptional. The wedding ceremony took place in the strictest privacy, according to a witness, William of Poitiers. William, accompanied by a fine escort of horsemen, also wished for his mother Arlette, his father-in-law Hellouin de Conteville and his two half-brothers Odo and Robert to attend. Matilda was accompanied by her father. There is no mention of the site where the religious ceremony took place and we are, to this day, unaware as to whether it was in the chapel of the Fortress of Eu, in the collegiate church of the same town or even in Rouen.

Obstacles facing the marriage

The Duke of Normandy's carefully orchestrated wedding plans were very soon to meet with serious opposition from Rome. During the council that was held in Reims in October 1049, "incestuous unions" were condemned and the Pope consequently forbade for the Count of Flanders to give his daughter's hand to the Duke of Normandy. Pope Leo IX's arguments against their union were based on genealogical factors. Matilda had Norman blood since she descended directly from Rollo. Furthermore, before marrying Baldwin of Flanders, her mother Adele of France was said to have been engaged to Richard III, Robert the Magnificent's brother, and therefore William's uncle. This union was not consumed, Richard having inexplicably and prematurely perished, but in the eyes of the church, this link was sufficient to establish consanguinity between William and Matilda, who were cousins and therefore incurred the crime of incest according to the church canons in force at the time. Most of the Norman bishops were present at the Reims council, including Hugues of Bayeux, Herbert of Lisieux and Geoffrey of Coutances. Lanfranc of Pavia, an Italian who had become Prior of the famous Benedictine abbey of Bec-Hellouin was also present. The reasons behind this formal opposition were mainly political. Pope Leo IX, already confronted with the Norman conquest in Sicily, was hostile to William. Furthermore, due to his Lorraine origins, he looked very badly upon the expansionist aims of the Count of Flanders who was in conflict with the Emperor of Germany. It should also be noted that the period between 1047 and 1048 was one burdened with many international conflicts. First of all, William the Conqueror defeated his rebellious barons at the battle of Val-ès-Dunes[5] on the 10th of August 1047; the Imperial Palace of Nijmegen in Holland was set on fire the same year by Baldwin of Flanders' soldiers. Finally, in 1048, the Norman Kingdom of Calabria, in southern Italy, was established by Robert Guiscard, son of Tancred of Hauteville. For the Pope, this was a step too far. Troubled by the increasing power of the Normans, he had to, at all costs, oppose the Norman-Flemish axis, even if it were to lead to excommunication.

5 Val-ès-Dunes is between Bellengreville and Chicheboville, two small towns approximately 10 kilometres to the East of Caen.

Revoking the anathema

The wedding took place despite opposition, but was yet to be acknowledged by the Vatican. Between 1050 and 1055, the Pope received visits from several church dignitaries sent by William to plead his cause: Robert Champart, Abbot of Jumièges, Jean de Ravenne, Abbot of Fécamp, Lanfranc, Prior of Bec-Hellouin. Lanfranc of Pavia was a clever man who knew only too well the Church's potential gain from such an affair. He was an evidently pious man and his frankness and talent conferred on him William's trust and friendship. On the death of Leo IX in 1059, Lanfranc obtained an audience with the new pontiff, Nicholas II, who was far less hostile to the Normans than his predecessor. The new pope waived the excommunication demanding in exchange the construction of four hospitals (at the time called "hôtels-Dieux") in Rouen, Caen, Bayeux and Cherbourg. As penitence to William and Matilda, he also ordered the creation of two abbeys in Caen, one for men – Saint Stephen's Abbey which was consecrated by Lanfranc in 1075, and one for women – the Holy Trinity Abbey. Some fifty years later, the chronicler Robert Wace recounts these events in the Roman de Rou,

" Par cunseil de sa barunie Prist une fame de haut lin En Flandres fille Balduin Mahelt out non, mult belle è gente... E li Dus iloc l'espusa... Puiz ont à Caem establies Mult richement dous abéies, En dui mostiers asez proçains, L'un à moignes, l'altre à nonains."

"Following the advice of his barons He took a venerable wife Daughter of Baldwin of Flanders Named Matilda beautiful and noble...And the Duke married her... Then established together in Caen Two richly endowed abbeys In two nearby monasteries One for monks the other for nuns."

"How the king, William the Bastard, after reconciling the country, had an abbey founded," William the Bastard and Matilda of Flanders visiting the construction site of the Caen abbey – such was the event that the 15th century *Chroniques de Normandie* chose to illustrate to depict this sovereign, whose support for the Church and whose defence of public order were greatly appreciated. (*Chroniques normandes*, 1410-1420, Rouen city library, ms y26 f° 101.)

The Ladies' Abbey, headquarters of the reunified Normandy Regional Council.

The abbey-church of St. Stephen.

The consecration of the Ladies' Abbey

On June 18th 1066, Duke William, Duchess Matilda and their children attended the consecration of the Holy Trinity Abbey in Caen, of which the construction had begun in 1052. They invited the most influential members of Norman society: the highest ranking barons and ecclesiastic dignitaries, bishops and abbots.

Diorama: Consecration of the Ladies' Abbey. Pewter figures made using the flat pewter technique and engraved in slate. By Alain Letort and Luc Marie.

Maurille, Archbishop of Rouen, presided over the ceremony. It marked a decisive period in Norman history, for William had, over the weeks prior to the consecration, begun to prepare a fleet of longships on the mouth of the River Dives, in view of the Norman Conquest of England. He was convinced that the consecration of the abbey would seal his agreement with the Church and facilitate his victory over the traitor Harold, who had usurped the English throne after the death of Edward. At the end of Mass, at the signature of the donation chart[6], William took his daughter, Cecily, by the hand and led her to the altar. The young girl was offered by her parents in oblation to the abbey, of which the first abbess was one of William's cousins named Matilda. Cecily was not the only young girl to join the Benedictine monastery; many other lords, wishing to emulate the duke, offered their daughter, sister or even mother in oblation, whilst endowing them with portions of their land. Among the countless signatures were those of Stigand of Mézidon, who gave his daughter and the benefaction of the three churches in Falaise, Raoul Taisson from Thury who gave 110 acres of land in Amblie for his sister, Roger of Moutiers from Courseulles, who gave land in Sallen and Vaux-sur-Seulles for his mother. Hence, around twenty young girls entered the order. Thanks to very rich endowments, the nuns were able to exploit watermills around Caen, in Gacé, Ecouché, Quettehou and Jersey, as well as land, saltworks, tithes on fishing and vines in Argences and Vernon. These considerable possessions, which were further endowed after the Norman Conquest, ensured the abbey's maintenance up to the French Revolution.

6 A chart is a solemn written statement from the ducal or royal authority.

The Ladies' Abbey crypt.

Her role at William's side

Once married to William, Matilda played an important role and was called upon by her husband to participate in key events, thus explaining the presence of her signature at the foot of many charts. Matilda's signature can be found on 20 among the 21 officially registered acts concerning the Caen abbeys. Her seal is also present on 30 of the 151 acts issued by William. She was also present during her husband's solemn lectures given three times a year at Christmas, Easter and Pentecost. These lectures reunited bishops, barons and abbots, and offered the opportunity to render justice and to make important decisions, initially concerning the duchy and, from 1067, pertaining to the whole kingdom. Throughout the rest of the year, an itinerant court travelled from castle to castle, depending on immediate political priorities; it was moved from Caen to Lillebonne, Rouen, London and other major towns. Far the most pompous was certainly the 1067 Easter court in Fécamp. William returned triumphant to his Norman fatherland after the Norman Conquest. He and his wife wore gold-encrusted robes; the crockery was of gold and silver as well as the beef horns used to serve abundant quantities of wine and whose extremities were plated with gold. However, the royal couple's favourite residence happened to be the Château de

Engraved stone from Barfleur: *"Aboard the Mora, Étienne from Barfleur took William to England,"* 1066.

The Mora, the ship Matilda offered to her husband, was adorned with a figurehead representing a child sounding a horn and reminding us that Matilda was expecting at the time of the conquest.

Caen Castle seen from the west ramparts with the barbican.

Bonneville-sur-Touques, which is where William officially endowed Matilda with the Regency of Normandy for the duration of his expedition to England. Matilda's period as Regent of Normandy, responsible for "the kingdom's wealth and authority," was quite considerate since not a single uprising, conflict or rebellion disturbed the duchy during the duke's absence. As Regent of the duchy, Matilda also played an active role in the preparation of the Norman Conquest. She armed the finest longship, the *Mora*, from her considerable personal fortune. On the 6th of December 1067, William set to sea again for England, this time taking Matilda with him. Two of their sons, Richard and William, also travelled with them, leaving Robert in Normandy to assure the Regency. The royal couple took up residence in London and this is very probably where their fourth son Henry Beauclerc was conceived. Then came the great day of Matilda's coronation, by Ealdred - Archbishop of York, in the Abbey Church of Westminster on the 11th of May 1068, the day of Pentecost.

Ruins of Fécamp Castle, one of the couple's favourite places of residence.

The entire kingdom's nobility was present, as well as Church dignitaries. Such was William's desire "since if God granted him this honour, he wished for his wife to be crowned with him." (William of Jumièges).

A fertile marriage

A successful union

Chroniclers and historians are unanimous in recounting that William and Matilda's union was a happy one. William, who was steeped in religious principles, was ever faithful to Matilda, as she was in turn to William. Despite the many and sometimes critical conflicts and uprisings they faced, their love for each other was everlasting. This was quite extraordinary in the Middle Ages and is, therefore, particularly worthy of note. In 1074, Pope Gregory VII addressed an epistle to Matilda, praising her good works,

"We do not believe that we should cast doubt upon the salvation of she who, with all of her heart, devotes herself to the Lord, by the exercise of deeds of charity and humility... Take continuous care to persuade the king, your husband to seek the salvation of his soul."

(Arch.Calv. 2H25/2, Trinity – Calvados Archives).

Let's take another look at the works of Robert Wace, the faithful chronicler,

"*Treiz filz out de li Robert, Guillame et Henri Dous filles out entre li filz Ele è Cécile mult gentilz.*"

"*She gave him three sons Robert, William and Henry Had two daughters between the sons Adele and Cecily, very kind ones.*"

In fact, Matilda had at least ten children.

Tree symbolising William and Matilda's many descendants.

William and Matilda

- **Robert** (1051 - 1134) Duke of Normandy
- **Richard** (1055 - 1075)
- **William II** (1060 - 1100) King of England
- **Cecily** (circa 1061-1127)
- **Agatha** (1062 - 1073)
- **Adele** (1068 - 1135) Countess of Blois
- **Henri I** (1068-1135) King of England
- **Constance** (deceased circa 1094) Duchess of Brittany
- **Adelise** (deceased before 1113) Nun at St-Léger-de-Préaux
- **Matilda**

The scenes represented inside the dropped initial B illustrate the destiny of William's sons: king or duke, warrior, hunter.

Many descendants

Man-to-man combat between Robert, Duke of Normandy, and a Muslim warrior, under the walls of Antioch. Oil on canvas by Jean-Joseph Dassy (1796-1865). Versailles, Palace of Versailles and the Trianon.

Robert Curthose (before 1051 - 1134)

Duke of Normandy from 1087 to 1106, Robert Curthose was the couple's first born, who William chose to name after his own father, Robert the Magnificent, lost during the Crusades. He was nicknamed Curthose: perhaps because of his smallness, or his liking for small ankle boots. This may even be an affectionate nickname given to him during his childhood. The mystery remains. One thing is certain; Robert Curthose was of a fiery temperament, and even as a teenager, sought conflict with his father by claiming his share of the inheritance. To which William is said to have sharply replied "I only lie down to sleep." The quarrel opposing William and his son appeared to be based on a conflict of generations, which William, having lost his own father at a very young age, was ill-prepared for. The truth was that Robert was ambitious and anxious to rapidly succeed William to the throne, to such an extent that he pledged allegiance to the King of France Philip I, his cousin, against his own father; an allegiance for which William was never to forgive him. Matilda, however, showed a certain weakness towards her "aîné-fils" (eldest son), to whom she was possibly more attached

than her other children, and secretly had money sent to him. On learning what he considered to be treason on the part of his wife, William burst into furious anger. Robert then took up a rebellious life, crossing swords with the entire duchy and conspiring against his father. On his death bed, William described him as a "proud and stupid ruffian". William's death left Robert heir to the Duchy of Normandy, while his brother, William Rufus acquired the throne of England. This inheritance was far from satisfying Robert's quest for power, and he instigated several expeditions to England, every one of them vowed to failure. Equally incapable of governing his duchy, which was plunged into chaos, he provoked the landing of William Rufus on the Normandy coast in 1091; civil war broke out throughout the duchy, which finally turned in favour of William, the English King. Robert sold the Cotentin and Avranchin regions to William Rufus for the derisory sum of 3,000 silver pounds! He was later to pawn the entire duchy to him by borrowing 10,000 silver marcs. Ultimately penniless and divested of his every possession, Duke Robert decided to accept Pope Urban II's call to join the Crusades. In the Holy Land, he joined the flower of French chivalry, Robert of Flanders, his cousin Godefroy de Bouillon, and his brother-in-law, Eustache de Boulogne. He also made acquaintance with Tancred, the Norman King of Sicily. In May 1096, he arrived in Constantinople and distinguished himself at the Battle of Jerusalem in 1099. On his return home he travelled via Puglia in southern Italy and married Sybil of Conversano, who gave him a son, William Cliton, in 1102. Back in his fatherland, crowned with honour and glory, Robert's first visit was to his mother's tomb, which lies to this day in the Ladies' Abbey in Caen. He met with his sister, Cecily a monastery nun, whom he shrouded with gifts. This wayward but sensitive young man had always

Robert Curthose. Oil on canvas by Henri Decaisne. The Palace of Versailles. The artist chose to represent him with Normandy's coat of arms. This is an anachronism for the leopards were only imposed by Richard the Lionheart.

preserved a certain degree of affection for this place that he had, not so long ago, defended against pillaging organised by his own brother Henry. A new civil war broke out in the duchy opposing the Normans and the English. Despite an agreement between the two brothers, signed at Alton, in England, their rivalry intensified, stirred by increasing disorder in the duchy - disorder which Robert Curthose was unable to contain, preferring to consecrate his time to debauchery. Henry I took advantage of the anarchy that reigned throughout Normandy and landed at Barfleur. Bayeux and the entire Bessin region surrounding the town were transformed into a blood bath of violent combat between the Duke of Normandy and the King of England, who pursued his brother as far as Tinchebray for the final battle. This battle on 29th September 1106 was to mark Robert Curthose's ultimate defeat. Henry took hold of Normandy, thus satisfying his effusive ambition. As for the ill-fortuned Duke of Normandy, suitably escorted to England, he was imprisoned in the golden jails of Cardiff and finally perished in 1134 after 29 years of captivity.

RICHARD (CIRCA 1055 - 1075)

William and Matilda's second son, born around 1055, was named after three Dukes of Normandy, the most famous being William's grandfather Richard II, known as Richard the Good who reigned from 996 to 1026. Like all young boys of the nobility, Richard was educated and trained to be a knight; he received instruction on handling arms, on horsemanship, hunting and falconry. He had a far more amenable nature than his brother Robert. His father, who was very fond of him, often took him on hunting outings, his favourite sport, in the royal New Forest in Hampshire. Alas, in 1075, during a hunting party, Richard was mortally wounded in an accident. This loss was a cruel shock to Matilda and heavily affected William, who became increasingly withdrawn.

WILLIAM
NICKNAMED RUFUS (CIRCA 1060 - 1100)

King of England (1087 - 1100). On his birth, he received the name of his father. William the Conqueror had chosen him to succeed to the throne of England. Once king, William Rufus shocked his English subjects by his attire, his long hair, and in particular, his inappropriate effeminate manners. On the 2nd of August 1100, he was tragically killed by an arrow during a hunting party in the New Forest, just like his brother Richard 25 years earlier: accident or murder? No one knows. However, it is said that his brother Henry, witness to the tragedy, turned back his horse and galloped fast and furious to Winchester to claim the Royal Treasure. Rufus was buried in Winchester Cathedral. No one mourned his death, despite the following verses on his epitaph by Baudri de Bourgueil,

Statue of William II Rufus - Canterbury Cathedral.

"Normans and English were seized with dread
Upon a simple nod of his head
And his generous hand cascading with gold
Loved to see his treasures unfold
Carrying the name of his father he knew
How to equal his noble deeds
First a consul, then king of high esteem:
Death came from an arrow fired to kill a deer
See how dies a great man!
His ashes are under the earth where we stand."

Cecily (circa 1061, before 1127)

Abbess of the Holy Trinity in Caen. Cecily was very young when her parents offered her in oblation to the Church on the 18th of June 1066, the day of the consecration of the Ladies' Abbey. Her entire childhood was spent among the monastic nuns until she pronounced her holy vows, devoting herself to God.

It was with Cecily that Matilda sought comfort when times were hard and she suffered from the death of her father Baldwin, the cruel loss of her two children Richard and Agatha, and the wayward escapades of Robert. It was therefore quite natural that Matilda should choose to be buried in the monastery where her daughter Cecily was resident. Cecily had already taken her holy vows when her brother Robert returned from the Crusades and visited the monastery, bringing with him many lavish gifts. In 1113, on the death of the first abbess, Cecily was chosen to replace her. Under her direction, the Holy Trinity Abbey was to develop an increased intellectual activity, the nuns composing verses of Latin and the abbey-church being adorned with its finest sculptures. Two other girls were born from William and Matilda's union, Adelise or Adelida, who became a nun in St-Léger-de-Préaux and who died prior to 1113, and Matilda of whom only the first name is known.

Agatha or Aelfgiva (before 1062 - circa 1073)

Agatha was named after Matilda's grandmother, wife of Baldwin IV of Flanders. It is said that Agatha is depicted on the Bayeux Tapestry in a scene where a clerk administers unction to her. She was but a small girl when William promised her hand to Harold, who, sent by King Edward, had sworn on the relics of a martyred saint that

Harold was promised Agatha's hand. This is one of the rare 11th century representations of a woman.

he would be faithful to William. We now know what followed. On Edward's death, Harold seized the throne of England and provoked the landing of William's soldiers at Pevensey. Harold was killed during the Battle of Hastings. Poor Agatha, who had originally been engaged to Herbert, Count of Maine, was then promised to the Spanish prince Alphonse of Léon. However they were never to marry for she died on a trip to Spain, it is said "*de fascherie*", (from anger), and her remains were brought back to France to be buried in Bayeux Cathedral.

Adele (1067-1137)

The poet Godfrey of Reims alluded to her birth as having taken place just after the Norman Conquest,

"From this Duke was born an admirable daughter...
So that a sceptre carrying king have Adele for a daughter
The Parcae wished for her father to be king
Thus, before the virgin saw the day
Her father owed her the throne of England."

No other documents allude to the date of birth of this child who was named after Matilda's mother Adele. But on reading the above verses, it would appear that Matilda was already pregnant when William left on his conquest to England. In 1080, Adele's father gave her hand to the Count of Blois in a splendid wedding ceremony. When her husband was killed during a Crusade in 1103, their son was too young to accede to the title of Count of Blois; it was therefore Adele who took on the responsibility of the Regency of the County of Blois. On the death of Henry Beauclerc in 1135, she endeavoured to have her son Stephen of Blois accede to the throne of England, then spent her last years in a convent in Marcigny, not far from Cluny in the Burgundy region.

The seal of Stephen Henry, Count of Blois.

Historiated initial "O", representing the ideal medieval couple. Bible of St. Bernard.

"Count Stephen sends to Adele, his sweetheart and spouse, the best and the dearest that his spirit may imagine. I have travelled well to Rome my dear, surrounded with honours and in good health. I have taken care to send you news of my travels and of my adventures by a scribe from Constantinople; however I fear that this messenger may have met with ill fortune, so I am writing this letter in my own hand. Thanks be to God, that I have joyfully reached Constantinople."

Letter from Stephen of Blois to Adele of Normandy, his wife, sent from the Crusades (19th or 20th June 1097). (*Lettres des croisades*. Académie des Inscriptions et Belles Lettres. 1866).

Henry I Beauclerc (1068 - 1135)

King of England (1100 - 1135), Duke of Normandy (1106 - 1135). Henry, who was given the name of the King of France, his great-uncle, was born in Selby in the English County of York. As the king's son, he was given a princely education, hence his nickname "Beauclerc". Highly literate, he was far from scorning life's pleasures and is said to have fathered some twenty illegitimate children. Hungry for power, he once questioned his father since he was astonished to only be promised a sum of money upon his death. William advised him to be patient, adding that his day would come. One can suppose that William foresaw the rivalry between his two sons over their inheritance, for in 1068, one year before his death, he knighted Henry in Westminster Cathedral in the presence of his entire Court. In 1100, upon the death of William Rufus who left no heirs, the throne was vacant. Henry saw this as an opportunity to accede to the throne, unless he had himself orchestrated the death of his brother, as his hasty return to Winchester to seize his throne would tend to lead us to believe. On Robert's return from the Crusades, his duchy was therefore governed by his brother, Henry, King of England. The combat between the two brothers, whose resources were unequal, came to an end at the battle of Tinchebray in favour of King Henry who permanently took control of the Duchy of Normandy. Henry Beauclerc was a pitiless man and sent his brother Robert to rot in the dungeons of Cardiff jail. The last years of Henry Beauclerc's life were plunged into mourning after the tragic loss at sea of his son William Atheling, born from his marriage with Edith of Scotland. The high sea shipwreck of the *Blanche Nef* (White Ship), off the coast of Barfleur on the terrible night of November 25th 1120 decimated the fine flower of Anglo-Norman aristocracy.

Henri I "Beauclerc", King of England. Extract of an illumination by Matthew Paris, *Historia anglorum.*

On Henry's death, the throne, which rightly should have been William Atheling's, was taken by Stephen of Blois, son of Adele, thus plunging the kingdom into a period of successive crises. Henry I Beauclerc left behind a portrait of a great king, a fine sovereign worthy of his kingdom, able to govern efficiently and to calm conflict. It was during Henry's reign that the Exchequer, a genuine kingdom revenue court, was set up.

"The riches of this world are of little importance
And offer nothing of precious value:
As proof King Henry who so treasured peace!
Was the richest of all western princes...
What a terrible night was the 1st of December...
That all England and Normandy now mourn!
For you are dead, Henry: throughout your life
These two nations knew peace, and now they know tears"
(William of Jumièges)

Constance (deceased in 1090)

She was given the same name as Matilda's grandmother, Constance of Arles, Queen of France. Constance was very close to her mother Matilda, who she accompanied to the Saint-Evroult priory and with whom she participated in the building's restoration. In 1086, she married Alan IV Fergent, Duke of Brittany, who joined Robert Curthose during the Crusades. Their marriage yielded no issue. She is said to have died imprisoned!

Matilda and the church

"The devil subjected by a bishop," chronicle by Julius Florus.

The main accounts of Matilda's life were written by the monks who knew her. Such was the case of William of Jumièges - royal chaplain of William's court and author of *Gesta Normannorum* (The Norman Deeds), of Orderic Vitalis - Prior of Saint Evroult and of Guy of Amiens – Matilda's personal chaplain. They unanimously praised Matilda's kind-heartedness and considered her to be a great queen and generous benefactor to the Church. History particularly bears in mind her donations to the Holy Trinity Abbey in Caen, which was the most richly endowed abbey of Matilda's era. But Matilda's liberality was not limited to the Ladies' Abbey. Her generosity enabled the reconstruction, from 1076, of the church of Notre-Dame de Guibray, which was previously too small to receive all of its faithful worshippers. Matilda's fondness of her husband's birthplace, Falaise, also gave way to important donations to its three churches: Saint-Laurent, Saint-Gervais and the Holy Trinity. Orderic Vitalis also spoke of a donation of 100 roumois[7] to restore the refectory in Saint Evroult, now in the Orne valley. Matilda also maintained correspondence with Pope Gregory VII, pontiff from 1073 to 1085, who appeared to appreciate William's support for the Church. This Pope, who was later to be canonised for the many reforms that he imposed on the Church, sent two epistles to Matilda, both overflowing with praise. In the second epistle, Pope Gregory wrote the following text,

"... *The most precious gift that we may desire from you ...for what gold, what precious stones could come within reach of the knowledge of your chaste and honest life, your charitable deeds to help the poor and of your means and the perfect love you give to the Lord and to your fellow creatures... We implore your Majesty to take all opportunities that God may give you to equip your husband with the same such arms.*"

Choir of the Holy Trinity abbey-church.

7 Roumois – currency coined in Rouen.

The Holy Trinity abbey-church,
today the church of St. Giles.

Regent of Normandy

Matilda was the King of France, Robert the Pious' granddaughter. Her royal blood, her culture and her personality were behind the exceptionally important political role she played for an 11th century woman. Matilda was one of William's most valued allies and he honoured her with his abiding trust. Matilda promptly committed herself to the destiny of the Duchy of Normandy and later the throne of England. Her regency, the presence of her signature on many charts and her coronation in London all bear witness to her involvement in political decisions and events. She played a front line role in the preparation of the Norman Conquest and obtained the discreet but efficient support of her father, the Count of Flanders, who was tutor to the King of France, Philip I, as yet too young to reign. Under Baldwin's influence, young Philip did nothing to oppose William's plans, and a division of French and Flemish soldiers even accompanied William's own at the Battle of Hastings. The Duchess of Normandy was also involved in naval construction, ordering the building of the finest vessels, capable of carrying some 600 men. The longship upon which William set sail displayed the papal standard, a golden cross on a silver background.

William of Jumièges and William the Conqueror: the monk and the king.

Church of Saint-Gervais in Falaise.

Church of the Holy Trinity in Falaise.

Matilda and France

Matilda's influence reached beyond the borders of the Anglo-Norman kingdom. She became acquainted with the Queen of France, Anne of Kiev whose son Philip and Matilda's own son Robert were of the same age and often played together. Their friendship was, however, to be detrimental to Robert's future relationship with his parents. On the death of Matilda's father, the Count of Flanders, his inheritance was to be handed down to Matilda's brother's eldest son, Arnould, then, upon the latter's death, to Baldwin. Matilda's younger brother, Robert the Frison, was hostile to such an inheritance and seized the title of Count of Flanders, much to Matilda's disapproval. Consequently, when the young King of France, Philip I solicited William's support in countering Robert the Frison, a small troop was dispatched, under the command of William Fitz Osbern. However, the ever determined Robert the Frison was victorious at Cassel on the 22nd of February 1071 where the faithful William Fitz Osbern met with his death. Matilda and William were thrown into dismay by this defeat which somewhat weakened King William's authority.

Below: Military preparations for the conquest: building boats.

Statue of Anne of Kiev in Senlis.

A tragic loss

In 1083, worn out by her numerous childbirths and tormented by the conflict between Robert and William, Matilda succumbed to an epidemic of Plague which raged through the town of Caen. She was barely fifty years old. She died on the dawn of the 1st of November, the day consecrated by Pope Gregory to celebrate all saints. William was severely affected by the death of "*the woman he loves more than himself*" and fell into deep depression which was to last until his death in 1087. In Matilda's will, she requested to be buried in the Ladies' Abbey where her daughter Cecily had become nun. She bequeathed to the Church "*her crown, her sceptre, the royal ornaments, those that she used to equip her horses, vases, cups, chalices in their cases, candlesticks made in Saint-Lô, gowns, belts, and other clothes some of which were tailored in Winchester.*" Her funeral was followed by an impressive procession of inhabitants from Caen, come to mourn their queen who had always cared for the poor. The entire region of Normandy was plunged into mourning and Mass was celebrated in honour of Matilda in the smallest and most remote of its churches. She also bequeathed all her belongings in England to her young son Henry.

"*The King dominated his enemies with arms, and you Matilda, you dominated them with peace. And your peace turned out to be far more efficient than was war.*"
(Godfrey of Cambrai, Prior of Winchester)

Queen Matilda's tombstone in the choir of the abbey-church.

Matilda's tomb

Matilda's grave is covered with a plaque of black Tournai Marble, reminiscent of her Flemish origins and engraved with an epitaph of thirteen Latin verses around the stone. The following translation was written by Michel de Boüard,

"This beautiful grave shelters with dignity
Matilda, of royal blood and of remarkable moral value. Her father was Duke of Flanders, and her mother Adele, Daughter of Robert King of France.
And sister of Henry who took seat on the royal throne.
United in marriage to the magnificent King William,
She founded an abbey and built this church,
Of so many lands and precious goods,
Endowed and hallowed by her will,
She was providence to the miserable, full of goodness.
Dealing out her treasures, she was poor to herself and rich to the needy.
Thus she gained her eternal dwelling,
On the first day of November, following the hour of prime[8]."

In the 18th century, the abbess of Tessé had Matilda's bones assembled in a lead box and ordered the construction of a new mausoleum, which alas, was destroyed during the French Revolution. In 1819, during the Restoration, the Calvados Prefect had a new tomb built, where Queen Matilda's followers have gathered and paid tribute to her to this very day. Matilda's grave has known many vicissitudes. It was originally an impressive mausoleum surmounted by her effigy, as was worthy of a great queen. In 1562, during the wars of religion, her grave was profaned by Admiral Gaspard of Coligny, chief protestant who took possession of Matilda's ring, a gold band surmounted by a sapphire. Madame de Montmorency, the convent abbess, demonstrated such reprobation and grief marked with profound dignity, that the admiral fell to his knees, imploring forgiveness and gave back the stolen jewel. The ring was given by the abbess to her father, Constable of France, a year later in the presence of King Charles IX.

Portrait of an abbess wearing Matilda's ring on her left hand.

8 In a Benedictine abbey, the office of "prime" is the first daily office celebrated in the early hours.

Legend and truth

William and Matilda's married life was source to many legends some of which have left their mark on the region's topology: hence the centre of Caen's "Rue Froide" (*Cold Street*), but also the "Cygne de Croix" (*Swan's Cross*), in the Rue de Falaise, rebuilt on the same spot as the "Croix Pleureuse", (the Crying Cross), depicting Matilda brutally dragged by her furious husband. Whilst the chroniclers at her majesty's service had always emphasised William's affection for his wife, such legends, supposedly based

Cadastre dating from 1825. Commune of Lassy where the legend of the "Cornu" is an integral part of topography. The Chapel "des Corps Nus" is located on the point inside the circle.

on truth, should be considered with caution. Certain tales in fact date from the 13th century, when Normandy was under the King of France's control. Indeed, after the Battle of Bouvines, an anti-English movement emerged and the once inflated image of the duke-kings was tarnished little by little. William was gradually considered to be irascible and violent towards Matilda, who was even suspected of having committed adultery. Historians, however, have never been able to confirm such a harsh relationship between the royal couple. Henri Prentout even spoke of the "*contamination of history by legend*".

These legends, however, bear witness to William's popularity and the appeal of the story of an illegitimate king who married a princess of nobler royal rank, a myth that exists to this very day.

The legend of their first meeting

"*Never in my life shall I marry a bastard,*" Matilda is said to have announced to her father. This cruel phrase was repeated to the Duke of Normandy, upon which he mounted his most faithful steed and raced across Normandy and Flanders to find his defiant beauty. He is then said to have beaten her before returning back to his Norman homeland. The young princess, captivated by such force and determination, then decided to consent to marriage with the duke.

La reine Mathilde travaillant à la Tapisserie de Bayeux, (Queen Matilda working on the Bayeux Tapestry) painting by Alfred Guillard (1810-1880), exhibited for the first time at the Salon de Caen fair in 1848 and currently displayed in the Baron Gérard Museum in Bayeux.

The legend of the naked body

On his return from the Norman Conquest, the knight Grimoult de Plessis, who had stayed in Normandy with the queen, reported to the king that she had been unfaithful to him during his absence. William, enraged, is said to have attached Matilda's hair to a horse's tail and dragged her naked through the streets of Caen. The terrified inhabitants barricaded their doors and shutters while poor Matilda cried "*My God, the Cold Street*[9]*!*" On their return to the castle, William had Matilda locked up in the dungeon. Suddenly, immersed in doubt, he put on a monk's robe and went to Matilda's cell to hear her confess her sin; their discussion revealed that Matilda had not betrayed William but that he had been the victim of a wicked conspiracy. The duke sought immediate and horrific revenge. He raced horsebound across the Suisse Normande and the Bocage regions and Grimoult du Plessis, who had fled, was rapidly captured by William's men who, slowly, after having attached his feet to a tree, like a rabbit ready to be skinned alive, tore his skin from his body with a wooden knife. The ill-fated "corps nu" or "cornu" (naked body) was finally quartered by four horses.

It is said that William kept the perjurer's skin under his saddle, such a trophy. Historical facts tell quite a different story. Grimoult du Plessis was part of a conspiracy against young William and participated in the Battle of Val-ès-Dunes. Following his overwhelming victory over his barons, William undertook to pursue them in order to inflict a ducal punishment upon them. Du Plessis was promptly captured and imprisoned in Rouen, where he was later to die. However, the 1825 cadastral survey of Lassy, in the vicinity of Montchauvet, reveals three hamlets whose evocative names are food for thought for amateurs of tales and legends: Hameau au Cornu, (Naked Body Hamlet) la Guairie (The Cured), and Ecorcheboeuf (Skinned Beef)...

9 The legend of a woman dragged by her hair also exists in England in the form of the legend of Lady Godiva in Coventry.

William giving orders to his messengers (left).
Harold taken prisoner by Guy of Ponthieu (right).

3.
4
S: EQUITANT: AD BOSHAM: ECCLESIA:
HIC HAROLD MARE NAVIGAVIT

The Bayeux Tapestry

For many centuries, the Bayeux Tapestry was said to be the work of Matilda who, just like Penelope, while waiting for her hero to return from his long voyage, embroidered his epic conquest. This is not true. Certain Latin words embroidered on the tapestry are of Saxon consonance, which is not suggestive of a Norman origin.

This magnificent 70 metre-long tapestry, is said in fact to have been financed by Odon, the Bishop of Bayeux and William's half-brother. He ordered the tapestry from the Canterbury embroidery workshops, in the English County of Kent, and it was given to Odon after the Conquest. The embroidery began as soon as William took the throne of England, and very probably ended some ten years later. We can, however, say with certainty that Matilda admired the tapestry on the 14th of July 1077, during the consecration of Bayeux Cathedral, attended by Matilda, William and their children. It was the first time that the tapestry was exhibited in the nave of the cathedral and admired by all. The Bayeux Tapestry, along with the Mont Saint-Michel is Normandy's most visited work of art. It tells the story of Harold's arrival in Normandy, of his perjury and the preparations for the conquest and the Battle of Hastings. It also offers a rich source of information on daily life in the 11th century with frescos depicting agriculture, hunting, meals, castles and churches.

Overall view of the Bayeux Tapestry.

Nave of the abbey-church of the Holy Trinity. Matilda's tomb is in the background in the church choir.

Zone Tertiaire de NONANT - 14400 BAYEUX
Tel: 02 31 51 81 31 - Fax : 02 31 51 81 32 - E-mail: info@orepeditions.com - Website: www.orepeditions.com
Editor: Grégory Pique – Layout and maps: David Thouroude – Editorial coordination: Kévin Decrouy
Translation edited by: Heather Inglis - ISBN: 978-2-9129-2581-7 - Copyright OREP 2016 - Legal deposit: 2nd quarter 2016

Photographic credits: Cover picture: statue de Mathilde au jardin du Luxembourg, lower cover picture: le Mora, © The Bayeux Tapestry, Town of Bayeux; p.2: (left) © the Bayeux Tapestry, Town of Bayeux, (right) © Archives départementales du Calvados; p.6: © the Bayeux Tapestry, Town of Bayeux; p.8: (up) © Coll. Bibliothèque municipale de Rouen – Thierry Ascencio-Parvy; p.9: © Michel Hourquet; p.11: © Gregory Wait; p.12: (up) © Michel Hourquet, (down) © The Bayeux Tapestry, Town of Bayeux; p.14: © the Bayeux Tapestry, Town of Bayeux; p.15 : © Coll. Bibliothèque municipale de Rouen – Thierry Ascencio-Parvy; p.16: © RMN; p.17: © RMN ; p.19: © The British Library Board MS Royal 14C, VII fol 8v; p.20: © The Bayeux Tapestry, Town of Bayeux; p.21: © Médiathèque de Troyes – Thierry Delcourt, © D.R.; p.22 : (ul) © Bibliothèque municipale d'Avranches ; p.23: © Michel Hourquet; p.19: (h) © Coll. Bibliothèque municipale de Rouen – Thierry Ascencio-Parvy, (d) © The Bayeux Tapestry, Town of Bayeux; p.25: (ul) © Jean-François Sehier, (ud) © Jean-François Sehier, (dr) © Office de tourisme de Senlis; p.26: © Région Basse-Normandie-Inventaire général – Manuel de Rugy; p.28: (r) © Archives départementales du Calvados, (l) © Town of Bayeux, musée Baron Gérard; p.29: © The Bayeux Tapestry, Town of Bayeux; p.30-31: © The Bayeux Tapestry, Town of Bayeux; p.32: © Gregory Wait; quatrième de couverture: © Michel Hourquet.